Working With Dads

7 Practical Steps to Engaging Fathers in Family Services

Sharmain Harris

Disclaimer:
In this book, the author will mention his employment time at WIC. WIC does not sponsor or endorse this book. They were simply the first employer to give the author a chance.

If you would like to purchase bulk copies of *Working With Dads, 7 Practical Steps to Engaging Fathers in Family Services* Contact us at **info@workingwithdads.com** for discount pricing.

1st edition, November 2021
ISBN-13: 978-1-7379926-0-8

Dedication

This book is Dedicated to every father who participated in my fatherhood program when I started it. It's because of you that I succeeded beyond expectations.

This book is dedicated to all of my colleagues who have supported me and my mission to fight for fatherhood.

This book is dedicated to all the practitioners around the world who are working on behalf of fathers and families.

Contents

Foreword

The panel on engaging men across child and family services was beginning to lose steam. It had been a long morning at the 'Labor of Love' summit in Indianapolis. And then it was Sharmain Harris's turn to speak. In minutes, I knew this was an authentic, fresh voice on the scene, speaking truth to institutions that had not always been so welcoming of him as a dad, especially with his history of incarceration. Absent was judgement and bitterness, and present was a voice urging us to join across our siloes to see men as the resource that they could be in the families with which we work – even the tough ones. What struck me was his straight talk about this complex problem, enriched by his careful attention to his own experience as the way to unlock a creativity that could help others.

That vitality has not dimmed since December 2016 and is on every page of 'Working with Dads'. From his own story of his awakening as a dad, he draws the reader into imminently practical conversations about how to engage men in settings that have for decades devoted themselves to serving the needs of mothers and their children, while inadvertently sidelining fathers with everything from their intake procedures to their therapeutic planning. His narratives draw the reader toward the inevitable conclusion that we have not been serving our families well by that father sidelining.

He gets down to business quickly, showing us in the table of contents that this book is full of steps, not chapters; steps that lead the reader to 'up his or her game' in father engagement. He includes helpful suggestions of conversation starters, a benefit often missing from books that focus more exclusively on theory or science. Not that he ignores the scientific foundation of successful father engagement; he references it when necessary, but never at the expense of that cherished practicality that we all appreciate when we start at the 'street level' to change our ways in working with families.

The book is an easy read because of its conversational style; one can almost feel the warmth of this man's engaging smile as you 'listen' to his beliefs, values, ideas, passion and compassion enrich every step. Step 6 is, for me, a clarion call to clinicians and workers in the family service world to roll back our biases toward addressing the needs of the mother-child pair at the expense of supporting the child's relationship with the father. This is one of the most cherished relationships we have in our lives, and supports child development like no other single intervention we can provide. Helping mothers make room for, support, and respect the unique role that fathers have in children's lives is so clear to Mr. Harris, that Step 6 represents some of the freshest thinking I have seen on this vital problem.

When you are done reading it, you will have your favorite Steps. I urge you to use this book more like a handbook than a text, make notes in the margins, underline and make it part of your own working curriculum. What he has to say will change the way you look at your next family.

Kyle D. Pruett, M.D.

3 November 2021

Northampton, MA

Introduction

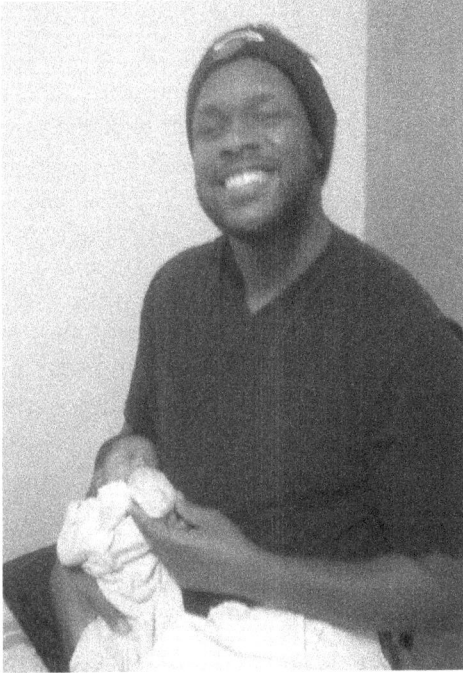

The boy that changed my life forever - My son Armani

In 2015, I walked into the local WIC clinic in Kenosha, WI. I was a new father walking in with my son who was about nine months old. Usually, I would have been at the WIC appointment with my wife but since she had to work and I was out of work from having surgery, I went to the appointment alone. After sitting in the lobby for a while, a lady came out and called out my wife's name. I figured out that it was indeed for us but since WIC stands for women, infants and children, the staff usually expect the mother to be at the appointment. When the WIC nutritionist saw that it was me she said, "Oh hey, Dad, how are you today?"

I let her know I was doing fine as I followed her to the back offices. While in the office, she checked my son's weight, height, and iron to make sure he was growing well. She then made some recommendations for my son. After finding out my son was in good health, the nutritionist began to converse with me. She asked, "Is this your first child?"

Excited, I told her that it was my first biological child but I also had an eight-year-old step daughter. She then asked how I felt and how things were going as a new father. I couldn't be happier that she asked. My mouth ran like a faucet as I talked about changing diapers, giving baths, and staying up late with him while my wife slept. I explained the mixed emotions inside me and my long term vision of providing for my son. She listened intently without once disrupting me. Outside of conversation with my wife, parents, and siblings, she was the only one that had engaged me on my personal fatherhood journey. I truly felt understood at that moment. After a short pause, she looked up to the wall at a flier. In a very excited voice, she said, "We are having a fatherhood event here soon. We are hoping to get a few fathers to come out for a meeting. We are trying to be more inclusive of fathers here at WIC and plan to have several activities now and in the future."

She told me there would be food and each participant will receive a gift card after the meeting. As a new dad, this event could not have excited me more. And mentioning food was a guarantee I would be there. I was already studying fatherhood, reading books on it, watching YouTube videos, and learning from the Bible. My father was not present for the early years of my life so I was eager to learn more about the early stages of fatherhood. I walked out of the WIC office feeling overjoyed. I immediately called my wife and let her know all about it.

Later, I learned that the purpose of the event was to ensure there was a need for fatherhood programming in the Kenosha area. A few days later, I showed up to the event thirsty for knowledge about fatherhood. I walked in and there was a large spread of breakfast items and hot coffee. Two men from an agency called the *Focus on Fatherhood Initiative* had come from Racine, WI, to host the meeting of fathers. They were both father involvement experts and facilitators. They were the only ones present when I arrived.

As we waited for more guests, we discussed topics such as discipline, co-parenting, and self-care. I began to open up more about my fatherhood journey. I let them know that I was a new dad and had doubts, fears, and anxiety about raising my son in this crazy world. The gentlemen gave feedback and told me they had the same feeling when they were my age. About thirty minutes into the session, the facilitators and I all seemed to look at the clock at the same time. One of the facilitators looked out the door and said, "I wonder if any other fathers will show?"

Although the WIC staff had been promoting this event for at least a month and expecting a great turnout. Unfortunately, it didn't turn out how expected

While taking a quick food break, the WIC clinic director walked into the room. I could sense the disappointment in her face and tone of voice. "Wow, only one guy," she said.

"Yes, it is unfortunate but this young man right here is on fire," said the facilitator in response. They let her know that even with one guy we were able to have some lively conversations. This is when I took action. I introduced myself to the WIC director and told her I was grateful for the event. I informed her that I wished I would have known about the event sooner and that I felt confident I could have gotten more fathers to come. I was well known in the community and everyone knew my father as well.

For some reason, I felt compelled to help. I offered to volunteer to host another event but with me as the host this time. This was something I was passionate about and I was sold on what WIC was trying to accomplish.

As we talked more, I told her that I could use my influence in the community to get fathers out who could really use the information. The director took down my contact information and said she would get back to me.

After about a week, she gave me a callback. I couldn't believe it. Although I offered to do it, a small part of me didn't think it would actually happen. We set a time to meet and do a small interview. While talking about myself and fatherhood, I felt more understood. After signing all the necessary volunteer forms, it was official. I literally told everyone immediately. I created a flier and posted it at all the local stores. I made digital copies and posted it on all of my social media outlets.

A few days out of the week, I was allowed to recruit fathers in the lobby of the WIC office and sign them up. I recruited and promoted the event for about three weeks and had a list of about fifty fathers. Although I had little experience in social work, I was becoming a rock star WIC volunteer.

In the days leading up to the event, I was super nervous. I did not expect things to move this fast. Talking to my father and my wife about it helped calm my nerves a bit, though.

In preparation for the event, I studied content from the *Nurturing Fathers Curriculum* to make facilitation easier. I also made sure I invited the facilitators from the previous meeting. I called, texted, and emailed all the fathers on my list constantly. I was expecting at least eight to ten fathers to show, but on the day of the event, there were well over twenty fathers rotating in and out of the sessions over a six-hour period.

The event was a success!

Seeing that, the WIC director and other staff were excited, especially since they had not been able to engage fathers like they wished to. After the event, I felt like I had accomplished my dreams. I couldn't believe I had pulled it off.

Shortly after the event, I had another conversation with the WIC director. To my surprise, she informed me that a potential job opportunity could spark from the event.

WIC was already in the process of seeking funding for a Father Involvement position specifically. She told me that I would be a strong candidate, especially after seeing the influence I had with the fathers at the event. She didn't make any promises but she said she would do her best to vouch for me.

I instantly called my wife and told her all about it. I wasn't even thinking this would turn into a career, I was just passionate about being a dad.

At the time, I was working for Red Robin Gourmet burgers as a line cook. While I was grateful for my job, securing a professional role sounded much more attractive than flipping burgers. Once I healed from surgery, I went back to work at Red Robin and patiently waited for the potential job opportunity.

The process was slow. Over a period of four months, I contacted the WIC director by email, phone, or stopping in at least once a week. Each time, she would tell me that the funding had not come yet, but it was coming. While we waited, WIC paid for me to be trained as a facilitator of the *Nurturing Fathers Curriculum*. I attended training during the first shift and went to work on the second shift. As I did the training, I became confident that the job was mine. Why would they waste money training me? But another two months went by and I began to get discouraged.

I started thinking that the nice lady just didn't want

to tell me no. I was sure that she did a background check and saw that I was a felon on parole and didn't want to move forward. So, for a while I gave up calling, emailing, and stopping in. If it was meant to be, it was meant to be. Then one day, I checked my email and it was the WIC director saying that they had secured funding for the positions. She told me to give her a call. I called immediately. I grinned as she told me they had enough funding to support my position as a Father Involvement Specialist for ten hours a week.

It wasn't much but enough to get my foot in the door. I came up with the name *Dedicated Dads* and started hosting fatherhood sessions twice a week. I used the rest of my time to recruit and input data. More funding came later through a minority health grant and I was eventually employed in a full-time position as a Father Involvement Specialist.

In my first year in the position, over 100 fathers completed the *Dedicated Dads* program. The movement took on a life of its own. The program filled a void in our small town of Kenosha, WI. We were the only organization making this kind of impact.

As the momentum progressed, the program began to be recognized both locally and nationally. Other WIC organizations requested for me to come speak to their staff. I began traveling to national WIC conferences to present as a keynote speaker. One year, we were invited to the Indiana annual labor of love summit. I shared the stage with child psychiatrist Kyle Pruett and the first African American Surgeon General Jocelyn Elders. Jerome Adams was the host but he would later become the Surgeon General during the Trump administration.

My life seemed so surreal and still does at times.

Since starting *Dedicated Dads*, I have helped over 500 fathers gain confidence and a sense of self-worth. The community has celebrated the wins of these fathers and my personal wins.

The *Dedicated Dads* program eventually received the Excellence in Community Action Award from WISCAP (Wisconsin Community Action Program). Shortly after that, I received the NAACP Positive Impact award, the Twenty Under Forty award, and the Young Leaders in Kenosha award. In 2016, the District Attorney helped me reduce my parole sentence by four years for my work in the community. The local news outlet covered this story with an article titled, "Making the Change - Former inmate now heads WIC program for fathers."

After the article came out, I was an instant celebrity. This is when fathers really started coming in. Most of them with similar backgrounds to mine and were in need of motivation and inspiration.

Around the same time, I received a full scholarship to Carthage College to study Business Management and Marketing. In May of 2021, I earned a Master's degree in Business Design and Innovation. If everything goes well, I will be receiving a pardon for my felonies from Governor Tony Evers in 2022.

As I continue to host groups, train organizations, and deliver keynote speeches, someone always asks me. "Sharmain, with all that you have been through, how did you accomplish all of this?"

My reply is always:

"Becoming a father."

Since realizing the effect being a father had on me, I've been eager to share with as many people as I can. While I didn't have many technical skills for recruiting and engaging fathers early in my career, I had a will. I had desire and passion. Those characteristics have been the key to my success in engaging fathers in a practical way. These practical methods are what I will be sharing with you in this book.

As fatherhood awareness rises, many organizations are seeking to engage fathers in their family services. They are being strategic in their approach and are focused on programming. But those programs do no justice if the staff does not know how to engage fathers from a holistic point of view. That is why I decided to write this book. Thinking back on my time at WIC, I think about how low father involvement was before I came along. I think about all the steps we took to successfully support the fathers we served. It was a perfect combination of strategy and practicality that took us from a grassroots organization to being known nationally.

Many of you reading this book are likely a part of an organization that has fathers coming in for services already. Maybe you have some kind of programming like employment services, job readiness, or child support prevention. Many of you probably already have strategies, funding, and resources for fathers, but your issue is engaging with fathers to get them to use what you are offering. This book will help you understand the mindset of fathers and therefore engage them more effectively which will increase enrollment in your programs.

Are you passionate and genuinely supportive of seeing families thrive?

Are you a leader in a social service organization that is tired of seeing broken families?

Are you someone on the frontline working with families every day? If so, you have picked the right book.

Whether you have been working in social services for decades, in the middle of your career, or recently finished your social work degree, by the end of this book you will be confident in your ability to not only engage fathers but become advocates for them.

Whether you work in child support services, corrections, or early childhood education, this book will give you a deeper understanding of fathers so that you can support the families in your services.

With the wide body of research available now on both the positive and negative impact of fatherhood; I'm going to assume you already have some surface level knowledge of its impact on families. This book will serve as a modern day guide for practitioners to develop confidence in supporting families. The time is now for us to step up and adjust to the modern day family. If not, we are going to continue to see generations of social ills rooted in the breakdown of the family structure. We will continue to see 85 percent of young males in prison due to a lack of fathers. We will continue to see 90 percent of homelessness due to a lack of fathers. We will continue to see 71 percent of teenage pregnancy as a result of fatherlessness.

Your role as a practitioner is crucial to the communities you live in. You don't realize it, but you may be the first person to support a family. You may be the first person to give someone a chance. I know most of you are not social workers but there is an element in your work. You may be the first person to actually listen to a family member and because of the information you provided they have an opportunity. You and so many other wonderful practitioners are on the frontline of serving families in your communities. You have to be prepared for every situation and can't leave any family behind.

I want to be very clear, while this book is focused on supporting fathers, it is not really about them. The ultimate focus is families and children. My hope is that this book will have an impact that will decrease the incidents of fatherless children for generations to come.

We know that kids do significantly better when raised in two parent households. We know children perform better socially, emotionally, and academically when both parents are involved. As service providers, we are in a unique position to make changes so that our next generation of leaders can flourish. These are our future teachers, politicians, and business leaders. It is our duty to do everything we can to prepare them. Supporting fathers in family services is one way to prepare them.

For the fathers who may come across this book, whether working in the field or just an everyday dad, this book will give you insight on how to get the most out of your experience in family service programs. Not only that, if you are a father that is eager like I am and can see yourself in this field, this book is for you. Social Services is 85 percent women. While that is not a bad thing, the field would greatly appreciate men like you being around. Your impact on families would be phenomenal.

As organizations start to recognize the value of fatherhood, they will not only involve more fathers, but hire them to add more diversity to their workforce. The knowledge and insight on fathers I will provide can help you to develop your own fatherhood movement ... if you choose.

The District Attorney and Judge releasing me from parole

Step 1. Understanding Fathers

"I came to understand the importance of fatherhood through its absence—both in my life and in the lives of others. I came to understand that the hole a man leaves when he abandons his responsibility to his children is one that no government can fill. We can do everything possible to provide good jobs and good schools and safe streets for our kids, but it will never be enough to fully make up the difference."

– President Barack Obama

For decades we have heard the narrative of the absent father in households. Societal issues played a major role in this narrative. Everything from wars, drugs, and mass incarceration. That along with the rise of divorce rates have been major factors in fatherlessness. Depressing stats about fatherless children have been long studied and researched. By now, we should know that children need both mother and father. If you listen to stories from your grandparents, you will learn that families went through some tumultuous times. Of course, we can't change the past but we can look toward the future.

Fortunately, there is a new paradigm for fathering in the new millennium. It is a shift from the older model of the distant, unavailable, uninvolved fathers to a more involved, emotionally and physically present father. Although there has been a paradigm shift in fathering, family services are still in the process of shifting. For decades, the welfare system has excluded fathers. Public assistance programs have been structured to focus on helping single mothers rise from poverty, but have overlooked the need to support the positive role of fathers. Not only for the impact they have on their children's lives but for the impact, they have on their entire family to succeed. The reason I start with this information is so you can understand why fathers are often hesitant to be a part of any services or even come inside your organizations. Even when they do come to your service, they are likely reluctant to engage. At the beginning of many of my Father's Engagement Training, I tell the story about WIC you just read about. I often ask for a volunteer to tell me what the acronym for WIC means. Women, Infants, and Children, right? What's missing? Obviously... Dad. Although the absence of Dad is communicated in their name, other organizations communicate this through their culture. So how could you possibly engage as a father when you consider all of that?

Engaging fathers in your programs and services is going to take some dedication and commitment. Especially when considering all the factors that potentially prevent it. The approach must be holistic in order to truly make an impact.

All right, so now that you have an understanding of fathers from a wide view, let's narrow it down by making it personal.

One of the first things we talk about in group sessions is the history of fatherhood for each father. A key part of the sessions is this section directly from the *Nurturing Fathers Curriculum*:

- We learn how to be fathers from our fathers or father role models.

- We tend to father the way we were fathered

- There is a powerful link between us and our fathers that should be acknowledged and respected.

- Even if our father was absent, his absence is part of who we are. There is an "invisible bond" that links us to the absent father and influences us as fathers.

- We are not condemned to repeat our father's mistakes.

- We can choose to be the father we want to be.

When we get to the part about the link and the invisible bond, I work hard to get the conversation flowing. At first fathers are unwilling to share their stories but as I open up about my story of fatherhood, they become more comfortable. As men share, both the physical and virtual rooms are filled with emotions. What we discover is that many fathers have resentment toward their fathers. Deep resentment. This is something that must be addressed if they are to be the fathers they need to be for their children. If this resentment goes unaddressed it can spill over to their relationship with their spouses and children. The reality is some of their fathers were absent, abusive, or emotionally distant. But when I ask them to think about their father's story they begin to understand. They discover that Dad's Dad wasn't present and sometimes Dad's, Dad's Dad. This goes into the generation of fatherless issues I was speaking on before. During this session, I over-emphasize the importance of addressing their fathering history so they can move forward.

In one of my sessions, I had both fathers and sons in the group. The older father was about forty-two and his son was around nineteen. After hearing from a few fathers, I asked the nineteen-year-old if he had anything to share. His father had not shared anything yet. The nineteen-year-old stood immediately to speak. This was surprising because young fathers take a while to speak up during a group but I guess he felt compelled that day. These aren't his exact words but it was something to the tune of:

"My dad has been in and out of prison my whole life, I feel like my life is destroyed because of that.

"My mom doesn't care about anybody but her boyfriend and is always kicking me out the house. I feel like I don't have anybody.

"I know my dad went through a lot, too, but he just can't seem to stay out of prison.

"Now I'm a father and I have no idea what I am doing, sometimes I think about just leaving my girlfriend because I can't handle all of this."

He spoke about his father as if he was not in the room.

Then he looked his dad in the eyes and started crying. I could tell it had been a while since he had a good cry. I started crying along with many others in the room. His dad walked up to his son and gave him a hug and the entire group surrounded him and his son. This was a true healing moment. That moment helped me truly understand the men I was working with. Most of the fathers I worked with have vowed to never be like their fathers. Others have used their father's mistakes as a reason to do the same. I remember one fathers saying:

"My father never bought me nice things, why should I buy my kids anything nice?"

Whichever way they decide to express the pain, the powerful link it there. One might say:

"My dad was an alcoholic… I will never drink" or they may say, "My dad was abusive, I will never abuse my kids." There is a powerful link that should be acknowledged and respected, even for the absent fathers. This session is always emotional.

This is important for you to know because the fathers you work with are dealing with fatherlessness themselves. I am not making a case that you need to be a counselor or anything; my only hope is that you begin to understand. I heard a quote one time that said, "It's hard to mistreat someone when you know their story."

When I was young, my mother and father went through a huge custody battle over me. During my early years, I would mostly see my father on the weekends. Then when I was about ten, he went to prison. He returned when I was about twelve. At this point, my father was making a major change in his life. Getting me in his custody was one of his goals. My mother, who was struggling to raise five kids alone at the time, wasn't doing too well. She always managed to care for us but I think the custody battle took a toll on her.

During the court process, I was forced to talk to guardian ad Litem's, go to court, and more. I hated this. Every time we would leave, my mother would be crying. I began to have a deep resentment for my father. When he would try to come pick me up, I would leave the house so I didn't have to go with him. When I knew he might show up to a parent teacher conference, I would make sure I was not there. Eventually, my father won custody and I had to move from my mother's house to my father's.

In the long run, this change of custody was good for me but I struggled through my teens. I had a negative view of my father and I believe this is why I rebelled so much during my teens. I got involved in gangs, drugs, and sex at an early age. I was a class clown in high school. And, although my grades were good, I earned a diploma and went to college, I still suffered from trauma and behavioral issues. The lack of a father early in my life led to resentment. That resentment was expressed through negative behavior.

I dropped out of college in 2008 and in 2009 I was facing years in prison for selling drugs. While in a military based boot camp program, we had to share a personal story of our upbringing. Along with other stories, I shared the custody process I just shared with you. As I shed tears thinking about my upbringing, I began to heal. Another exercise we did was ask our parents to write us letters about how our decision impacted their lives. My mother wrote one of the most profound letters and the level of transparency in my father's letter brought tears to my eyes. I realized that my parents made the best of the resources they had available to them. I began to understand. I had to read these letters in front of twenty other men. Tears dripped on the ink of the pages as I tried to get every word out. It was at that moment that I identified my trauma. That moment was the start of me becoming who I am today.

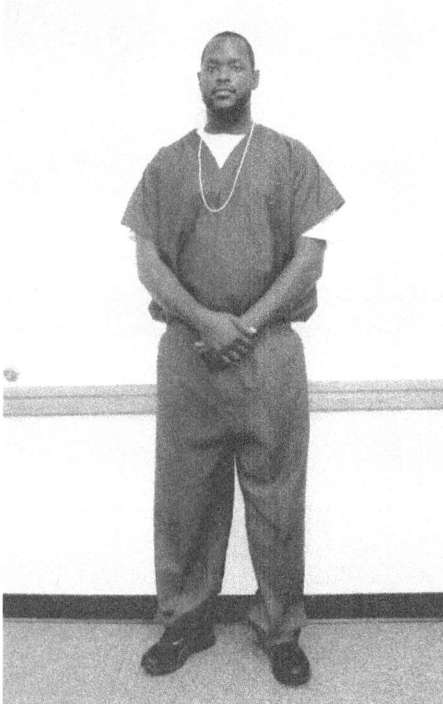

Serving time in prison

I hope my story and those of others helped you understand the complexities of fatherhood. Understanding the history of anyone will help you understand their actions. Many relationships fail because those involved either don't share or feel uncomfortable sharing their history. It may not seem like it but we engage in professional relationships with the families we serve every day. Having just a small amount of emotional intelligence will take your professional role to the next level. Emotional intelligence is a tool that all social workers can benefit from.

What is emotional intelligence?

The term emotional intelligence was created by two researchers, Peter Salavoy and John Mayer, in their article "Emotional Intelligence" in the journal *Imagination, Cognition, and Personality* in 1990. It was later popularized by Dan Goleman in his 1996 book, *Emotional Intelligence.*

Emotional intelligence is the capacity to be aware of, control, and express one's emotions, and to handle interpersonal relationships judiciously and empathetically.

"Emotional intelligence is the key to both personal and professional success."

Daniel Goleman gives four major areas to focus on to be emotionally intelligent.

Self-Awareness

Self-Management

Social Awareness

Relationship Management

The story I told and the stories of others focused on Self-Awareness and Self-Management. As I became self-aware of my history, I was able to manage myself. This is the same for the fathers involved in my programs. This is the same for the fathers you serve. But helping them get to that point is the challenge. We will talk more about getting them there in a later chapter.

Let's zoom in on Social Awareness and Relationship Management.

As I help fathers uncover their fathers' story they begin to at least understand their old man. They also talk about the social setting of their fathers. Unfortunately, most of their fathers have a history of incarceration. And like me, the sons ended up being incarcerated as well. When we dig into the history of incarceration, fathers become socially aware. According to The Sentencing Project, the United States is the world's leader in incarceration. There are 2.3 million people in the nation's prison and jails - a 500 percent increase over the last forty years. Changes in sentencing law and policy, NOT changes in crime rates, explain most of this increase.

Forty years brings us to the 80s and 90s which was a trying time for many families. There were so many political and systemic factors that disenfranchised inner city communities. Michelle Alexander, author of *The New Jim Crow: Mass Incarceration in the Age of Colorblindness*, does a brilliant job in explaining the negative long term effects of policies and systems of those times.

There's also a Netflix series called "13th" that breaks down the prison for profit industry and how big business uses the government to keep jails full. This book is not about that but it's something you should be "socially aware" of. The twenty-five-year-old fathers we engage now are the sons of those impacted by incarceration rates. After years of working with this group, I can honestly say that they benefit the most from family support programs.

Another force you should be aware of is family court. Family courts don't have the best track record when it comes to bringing families together. In fact, family courts often break families apart.

In the book, *Fathers' Rights* by Jefferey Leving, he states:

> "Until about twenty years ago, custody for divorcing a couple's children was, by statute, awarded to the mother. The 'tender years' doctrine,' family law for more than 100 years, required that young children (of tender years) be kept with the mother after divorce. The basis of this mandate was the widely held belief that women were more 'naturally suited' to parenthood than men. It was not until the early 1970's that a political commitment to racial and gender equality forced the repeal of the tender year's doctrine. Unfortunately, the overt gender bias inherent in the concept has survived to this day. Now, new custody laws enacted around the U.S. declare that the 'best interest of the children' be the primary consideration in custody decisions."

What attorney Jefferey Leving is referring to is the tender year doctrine.

The tender years' doctrine was a legal principle in family law since the late 19th century. In common law, it presumes that during a child's "tender" years (generally regarded as the age of four and under), the mother should have custody of the child. The doctrine often arises in divorce proceedings.

I believe that when laws like these were created they may have been necessary. America's history of War, the Great Depression, and Industrialization has impacted many families. Families during those times went through trauma and fathers spent more time away from the house than ever before. But as I mentioned before, there has been a shift and fathers are more involved. Honestly, every area of American culture has evolved and it always does.

Unfortunately, the courts have not changed. Family and criminal courts tend to be traditional and very conservative. Fathers often suffer the most because of this mindset. For years fathers have been incarcerated for missing child support payments. There is no statistical evidence that this concept works. Mothers often take advantage of court rules to keep fathers away from their children. Fathers are refusing to pay child support thinking it will help them see their children but they only end up in jail again.

Here is another excerpt from *Fathers' Rights*:

"A father's refusal to live up to his child support responsibilities cannot be defended, condoned, or rationalized. In many cases, however, a father's emotions, and not his character, rule his actions. Many estranged fathers believe that withholding of child support is the only weapon they have to counteract the banishment, visitation obstruction, harassment, and alienation suffered at the hands of former spouses. Unable to obtain relief for legitimate grievances from biased or uncaring family courts, these fathers, essentially, are trying to use support funds to buy parenting time. It's a desperate measure by desperate men."

You may be wondering what this has to do with engaging fathers. It has everything to do with it. Raising your emotional intelligence around social awareness with fathers allows you to speak directly to their hearts. Sometimes just nodding in agreement as they vent will increase your credibility. As the father grows confidence, his family grows as well.

As I became aware of how things work in the courts, I started working hard to help families avoid them. They are not a family service like us. They are just there to rule. As family service providers we have more contact and impact on families. If I could get a couple to join a co-parenting session or at minimum be cordial with each other, I feel accomplished. If it gets to a point where I must refer a father to legal counsel, I know it won't end well.

I became even more socially aware as I went through the certification process to be a family mediator. The facilitator made a comment that made so much sense to me.

She said, "When working with divorcing couples, you are dealing with people that at minimum have been together for three or more years. They know each other more so during mediation spouses may no longer like each other but have mutual respect. The process of sharing child placement is a bit smoother than unmarried couples. With unmarried couples, it is quite possible for the couple to be young and have not known each other for more than a year. In custody hearings, they both hate each other and don't trust one another. Getting to an agreement on child placement is rough because if they don't trust each other they don't trust the other parent to take care of the children."

Knowing this increases my efforts to keep young couples together. Then I discovered that on average, first time parents between the ages of 17-25 tend to break up after the baby is about eighteen months of age. In later chapters, you will learn why we decided to target this group at WIC.

Understanding dads has everything to do with being socially aware. As you learn about the wider view of the history of fatherlessness, you begin to understand. As you look at individual scenarios like mine, you take a deeper dive into your emotional intelligence. As you realize the circular economy and how systems affect everything, your way of operating changes slightly. My hope is that the information I've shared with you supports your efforts in engaging fathers. You don't have to be a father yourself to understand them but you do need to be aware.

As much as I am aware of fatherhood struggles, I am aware of mothers' struggles as well. Single mothers make up 80 percent. That information only gives me more fuel to work with fathers in the hopes of strengthening families.

As you continue your work in family service, remember that the simple act of understanding fathers will help make you an expert in engaging fathers and building families.

Step 2. Effective Communication with Fathers

"Communication is only effective when we communicate in a way that is meaningful to the recipient, not ourselves."

- RICH SIMMONDS

Now that you have an understanding of the fathers you will potentially engage, you can think about communicating with them. Obviously, it's easy to just go up and say some words to anyone but this chapter will teach you how to communicate better with them. In this chapter, you will learn about how to control implicit bias, how to make your environment father-friendly, and how to spark conversation with the fathers in your social services.

To begin, let's look at an example by looking at a scene in a movie about fatherhood.

Recently the movie *Fatherhood* was released on Netflix. It's an American comedy-drama film directed by Paul Weitz from a screenplay by Weitz and Dana Stevens based on the 2011 memoir, *Two Kisses for Maddy: A Memoir of Loss and Love* by Matthew Logelin. The film stars Kevin Hart and follows a new father who struggles to raise his daughter after the sudden death of his wife. It's a great movie to watch. There was a scene that caught my attention though. As Kevin Hart or "Matt" navigates life as a single father, he attempts to attend a parenting group to get support. He is having a hard time dealing with the constant crying, stooling, and throwing up of his daughter. When he opens the door a woman speaks up and says, "I'm sorry AA (Alcohol Anonymous) is down the hall."

Matt brushes it off and tells her that he is not there for that and proceeds to bring his baby into the room. After frantically describing his frustrations and begging for support the woman states, "I'm sorry but this is a group for new mothers."

Matt replies by saying, "You're lying; the sign outside says parents," then continues to explain his situation. While the scene was meant to be funny, situations like these are quite the reality.

The women in the movie didn't even ask where the mother was. She didn't care to discover what the father's true needs were. To be honest, the women did not even care about the needs of the child. She was blinded by a biased mindset on gender roles. Once she removes the blinders, she will realize that helping any parent helps the entire family.

In that scenario, the father could have been discouraged and started to think ALL parent services are like that. If his wife was alive, he could have told her that she needs to go to any appointments alone because clearly, it's not for men. I'm being extreme here but these are real possibilities. Now you have a stressed-out mother at the appointment upset that she had to carry a thirty-pound baby alone up a flight of stairs.

I know I said this before but I can't stress this point enough: The work we are doing is not about the adults, it's about the children involved and the impact we will have on their future. By supporting both parents, we support the entire family. The quote below drives this point more:

"Helping women and not men creates huge gender asymmetry, which makes it harder for couples to stay together," said Harvard sociologist Kathryn Edin, author of *Doing the Best I Can: Fatherhood in the Inner City.*

With that in mind, let's start by focusing on our mindset. I told you before how WIC had plans and strategies before I arrived and added passion and practicality. A big part of their strategy focused on training staff. In the early phases, they hired someone to train their staff on the process of engaging fathers. A key part of the training was on implicit bias. If you ever took the Harvard Implicit Association Test, you are aware that our society breeds implicit bias. This training focuses on staff's attitude toward fathers and the different kinds of fathers. Especially since over 80 percent of social service workers are women.

Essentially, the training helped the mainly female staff dive into their own history of fatherhood and how it can impact their work. Also, how a terrible divorce process could force someone to view all other ex-spouses the same.

In Chapter 1, I talked about understanding Dad and his history of fatherlessness. The same thing applies to young girls. They have deep seeded stories as well that affect them in the long term.

As professionals, you must be able to separate personal from professional. Sometimes relationships go through a rollercoaster and days are good and bad. If a father catches you on a bad day and you carry personal over to a professional, it could scar your organization.

The training did a great job for my WIC co-workers. I remember one of my co-workers going through a divorce after a long marriage. We would often share personal stories with each other. I was fascinated at how she kept up her pace with engaging fathers. She didn't miss a beat and continued to be enthusiastic.

Another co-worker had been through a divorce previously. She did not let that get in her way of communicating with fathers. She was what I call a fatherhood champion. She was a key to our FIT team (Father Involvement Team). Our team met monthly to establish goals and keep fatherhood a priority in the minds of other staff. She always had the greatest ideas, she volunteered at all the events, and the fathers knew they could approach her anytime. She would recruit so many fathers, I had to slow her down sometimes. Still to this day, she refers fathers to my program or gives them my information for support.

Trust me, I know separating personal from professional is challenging. A few times, I have prejudged fathers and assumed things about them. At one point, fathers were referred to my program from probation and parole. I could always tell when they were only attending to avoid trouble because they wouldn't take things seriously.

I had to separate my personal experience of dealing with parole from my professional experience of dealing with it. I couldn't judge. Although I could tell they were not taking the group seriously, I did not let that limit the way I engaged them or limit the resources I provided to them.

Remember the acronym P.I.E.(Person In The Environment). The clients you work with are often dealing with issues in their environment. They come from an environment that may not communicate like we do as professionals. This is where your emotional intelligence thrives. We talked about social awareness and relationship management in the previous chapter. This is where self-awareness and self-management is important. You must be aware of your personal story and the role it plays in your life. What biases do you have? How have you addressed them? What makes you tic? We all go through it.

Again, remember P.I.E., and always remind yourself that each father is not the same as the last father you worked with, whether it was a good experience or not. We must be self-aware so we can then manage ourselves. Sometimes you may need another coworker's support to help a family. You may need examples of how things were handled in the past. Recognizing this is what emotional intelligence is all about. This slight shift in your mindset will lead to a cultural change and your services will be seen as father-friendly.

Environment

So now that we discussed mindset, let's talk about the environment of your family service.

Did you know that the environment speaks volume to the families that come in your services?

Just like other businesses, the setting influences the customers. When you go to children's hospitals they have very bright colors and pictures to brighten the spirit of sick kids. When you go to a bank the colors are more neutral to communicate the emphasis on business.

What does the environment at your family service communicate to the families you serve?

When I took on the volunteer role, I was eager to succeed. My recruiting methods were above and beyond. A few times, I irritated some families because of my persistence. This one day I was recruiting in the lobby. I saw an all-black truck pull up outside the front windows. A family of four began exiting the vehicle. A mother, father, toddler, and a baby. The father got out of the driver's seat to help get the baby out while the mom helped the toddler. I was excited, as always, when a father came into WIC. Suddenly, I saw the dad go back to the driver's seat as the mother and the kids walked into the office. I thought to myself, "Dang it, about to miss another father."

So far I had only approached fathers that were waiting in the lobby. I thought about going out to the car. Then I did. I walked to the passenger window and said, "Hey what's up, man, you know you can come in here also, right?"

He could barely hear me so he got out of the car and walked to the sidewalk. I explained to him again that he is more than welcome to come inside. That's when he said, "Oh, I thought this was only for the mom and the kids." I lit up inside at the thought of changing this guy's mind. Eventually, I brought him inside and took him to the room his family was in. He later joined the fatherhood program.

I shook my head as I pondered how this father hadn't even been inside and he thought the service was not for him. This was something I wanted to work on immediately. In the early stages of working, I bought a training course from the National Fatherhood Initiative (NFI) to be a certified Father Engagement Specialist. The training talked about creating a father-friendly organization with pictures, signs, flyers, and more. Outside of the breastfeeding area, the lobby at WIC had nothing that communicated to fathers. I purchased several posters from NFI and hung them up around the office. Most of them had the words: "Have you been a father today?" with a positive image of a father and child. NFI has a diverse selection to choose from. I used every race available to make the WIC environment more father-friendly.

I also purchase a variety of 3x8 fatherhood bro-chures to give away to fathers. After a while, I got a cubicle area that was visible to every family that came in. I bought some big, bold letter cut outs and tacked the word FATHERHOOD to my picture board.

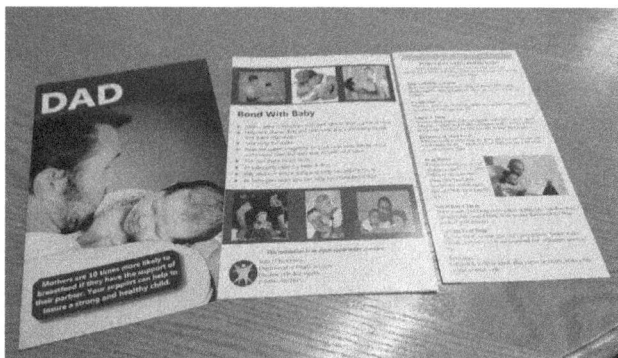

Marketing Material from the National Fatherhood Initiative

Engaging fathers became much easier after that. I would just wait until I saw a father looking at one of the posters and approach with a smile and say, "Have you been a dad today?" Almost immediately they would smile and point to their children.

I am hoping that as you process this information that ideas start to generate for you.

What message do you think your current environment is communicating to fathers?

How can you take these practical steps and apply them to your setting?

What resources do you need to enhance marketing material?

Your family service environment speaks directly to anyone that comes in. People pay attention to it all. I can't count how many times I got compliments from mothers and fathers on my personal family photos on my desk. The same goes for other staff as well.

All right, now you know how to control your bias and shape your environment. Let's wrap this chapter up with some conversation starters you can use right away while engaging fathers. These conversation starters are organic to the point you can slide them into any conversation.

Believe it or not, people love talking about their kids. You may have a coworker who won't stop talking about their kids. The reality is, having children is a major event in our lives so when the topic comes up, we tell our stories. When I would approach dads, I would go directly to talking about the kids. Never mind the small talk of "good morning and how are you?" I go right in as I approach them.

"Wow, that's a healthy baby… How old is he/she?"

When they tell me the age I quickly find a way to relate. As I said, when I started my son was an infant as well. So I might respond with something like: "Yea, man, I got an eighteen month-old myself, he is about twenty-five pounds now." Then I would set up for another question.

"It's crazy, he was only seven lbs. when he was born and he is growing like crazy… How much did your baby weigh when he/she was born?"

Generally, the conversation will take on a life of its own after that. But what's happening is that a personal relationship is being established with the father. Even if the father did not join my program at that moment, he remembers me being personable and approachable. Oftentimes, I would engage a father in the lobby and they wouldn't respond as I thought they would. But a week, month or even a year down the line they contact me.

Another way is talking about sports. If you've ever been in a relationship you know that some people love their sports. This is another lesson in social awareness. If you see a father walk in with a Packers hat on and you know the Packers just won the night before, that is a perfect way to spark conversation.

My workspace at WIC. Notice the Packer clock and the word FATHERHOOD boldly presented

Even if you didn't actually watch the game there is nothing wrong with saying something like:

"Great game last night, right?" They will light up and start talking. You can use this to segway into more pertinent questions.

This could also work if their team lost and you like the other team. You could make a slight dig on their team. Most fathers are not overly sensitive so they are not going to get upset. I would always pick on fathers that were Bears fans when the Packers beat them. They smiled every time.

Here are a few more questions you can use. Keep in mind that the person asking the questions is directing the conversation. These questions are not for you to get off track and only talk about them, they are used to guide them into the information you really want them to know.

Is this your first child? (even if it's evident, still ask the question to build rapport.) This is mainly for services being provided to families with children 0-5.

What has your child taught you since becoming a father? (This could be used in an educational setting. Maybe a parenting program at a school.)

What habits help you and mom raise your child better together? (Could be used in a child support service/co-parenting program.)

In this chapter, we discussed how to communicate with fathers. You learned how emotional intelligence plays a crucial role in your work as a social worker. You also took a deep dive into implicit bias, which we all have. You learned how to control your personal biases. Notice I did not say "get rid of" but control. Now all you need to do is take the examples and tools I provided you and use them in your family services. You will be surprised at the results.

Step 3. Supporting Fathers

The nature of impending fatherhood is that you are doing something that you're unqualified to do, and then you become qualified while doing it."

–John Green

You are well on your way to becoming a father engagement expert. You understand them, you know how to communicate with them, now let's learn how to support them. The way you support fathers will depend on how your organization serves families. Family issues are both deep and wide. You will need to be specific on how you want to support fathers in your organization. For example, here are a few questions that leaders involved with early head start may ask:

Is early childhood education a high need in your area? How could engaging fathers support babies that have been identified as needing more support?

What is the data on third grade reading levels in your region?

What does the research on the impact of early childhood intervention say? How could you impact the socioeconomic status of your community ?.

What is the demographic breakdown of the mothers you serve already? How many fathers come in with the mothers at appointments?

How could engaging fathers impact the overall outcomes of early childhood education on a macro level?

These questions can be applied to a wide range of causes. Maybe the need in your area is homelessness, teen pregnancy, or juvenile delinquency. Perhaps it is domestic violence or foster care. On a lighter note, you could be a religious group that wants to increase the number of fathers as chaperones on summer camping adventures.

This is something you and other leaders of your organization have to think about. You are already doing a great job with your services; it's just a matter of being more inclusive. Increasing the amount of family participation will amplify the good you already do. You will only improve and increase the amount of participation when engaging fathers in your family services. This framework will help you decide how you want to support the fathers. Is it programming? Is it a small activity? Is it home visitation activities with dads involved? Or are they large annual events? When you are being specific while engaging fathers, keep in mind that you are always supporting the entire family.

Before I got involved with WIC, they had already done an extensive amount of work to discover the need for father involvement and how engaging fathers will ultimately support the entire family.

Father involvement was identified as a priority by an organization WIC was collaborating with, the Kenosha Life course Initiative for Healthy Families or (KLIHF). KLIHF aimed to address one of the most perplexing disparities in Wisconsin - African American infant mortality. The collaboration was designed to improve conditions that promote healthier birth out-comes among African American families in four communities - Beloit, Kenosha, Milwaukee, and Racine.

Nearly all states have racial disparities when it comes to infant mortality, but Wisconsin has the nation's highest gap between white and black babies. So much so, it's worse than some third world countries. According to infant mortality data compiled by the CDC's National Center for Health Statistics, the rate of infant deaths for black babies in Wisconsin is nearly three times as high as white babies. Based on those stats and the high caseload of African American women with kids from 0-5, we determined where our focus should go.

According to research done by WIC, the Women, Infants, and Children (WIC) Program in Kenosha had a monthly caseload of over 4,100 women and children at that time. African Americans comprised 20 of that number. Unduplicated participation was generally around 2,000 women, over 1300 infants, and almost 3,500 children under the age of five. High incidents of infant mortality was the foundation for engaging more fathers. We began focusing on fathers and it eventually turned into a comprehensive program. The idea was that if we can communicate the causes of infant mortality to both parents and educate them on preventative methods to minimize them, we would have an impact.

When I joined the team, I remember meeting with my supervisor about the issues. She was on the board of the child death review board. It was discovered that seven infant deaths happened in less than two weeks. The deaths were spread between Kenosha, Racine, and Milwaukee. Some of the causes were SIDS (sudden infant death syndrome), co-sleeping and some cases were pure negligence.

Shortly after that, a newspaper article came out about a young couple who made a terrible mistake in communication about feeding their child. According to the article, the mother went to grab a water bottle out of the refrigerator to use for mixing the baby formula. It was late, she was a new mom so she didn't inspect the bottle. Sadly, the father had taken the water bottle, poured out its content, and filled it with vodka. It is a terrible situation to say the least. Fortunately, the child was only hospitalized and did not die. That story stuck with me all while I worked and still does to this day. Was this bad parenting? Maybe, but it really displays the need for education about co-parenting and communication. Every time I had a co-parenting session, I would bring up this scenario and ask the group how they could have handled it better. The number one answer was communication. So to bring it back, decreasing the number of infant mortalities and providing support for the African American families we served was at the top of our priorities when supporting families.

Our mission for this initiative became "To strengthen and build families through father involvement." The families we served needed strength and structure. We accomplished this through engaging fathers and father-specific programming. It was decided that supporting fathers with long-term programming was the best way to engage fathers. During that decision process was when I came along - as I talked about in the introduction. I was trained in the *Nurturing Fathers Curriculum* and started the *Dedicated Dads* program.

What may be the highest issues, cause, or disparity in your area?

How might you support families even more by being intentional about fathers' involvement?

How might you make a case to be more inclusive of fathers in your family services?

This is a challenge. We know that there are situations where parents are no longer together or relationships have ended. This is where engaging fathers takes on a broader meaning. You can focus on engaging fathers while keeping in mind that some mothers will come in with brothers or even their fathers. As long as there's a man present, we can consider engaging him.

We also must consider the single fathers that utilize family services. If single fathers don't feel they can come to your services because they are no longer with mom, we miss out on an opportunity to support the children in his care.

As you choose how you will support fathers, begin to think about resources you can provide them. You may not have the resources to do father-specific programming but you can refer them out. You may only want to be more inclusive and friendly to fathers but you can still be seen as a source of information. Some fathers may not be interested in what you offer but instead need information for other areas of their lives.

Here is a list of common resources I've provided for fathers:

Child Support Services - This one will be a big referral. In fact, when I first started *Dedicated Dads*,

I immediately built relationships with child support services. I got a child support question so much that I started to invite child support staff to meetings once a month. We eventually established a partnership to provide fathers with group services while they focused on job training.

Mental Health Services - I remember inviting a therapist into one of our sessions. As she went through the list of mental disorders, one of the fathers stood up and asked, "Is it possible to have all of these mental disorders at once ?" We laughed but he was really serious. We got them connected and although it's with a different provider, the father still attends therapy to this day.

Food Pantries and Shelters - An academic study was conducted on the fathers at WIC. A focus group revealed that food insecurity was the number one need for the fathers surveyed. Followed by financial literacy and employment. Food insecurity for fathers is real. Many of them don't qualify for any assistance because they are non-custodial fathers. If these kids don't live with them, the income they make is based on feeding one person. Since most benefit programs use gross pay to determine eligibility, child support deductions go unnoticed.

Legal Advice - As it relates to child support, fathers may need support with legal counsel. Having connections with organizations like Legal Action will support fathers. Most of my referrals are for this. The community started calling my "that father's rights guy" but that was not the case. I was just efficient in referring them to resources and walking them through the process.

This is another thing to be socially aware of. Fathers may not come for the direct services you offer but for the support service. By supporting fathers, you are supporting your services and supporting families.

Job Training and Employment - Of course employment is always needed. Not just any employment but gainful employment. Be aware of any job fairs taking place in your area.

Be very knowledgeable about the resources in your community. You may even create a list and add them to a pamphlet you can pass out to those seeking resources.

To wrap this chapter up, I want to share another story. Around the same time as the string of infant deaths, another story came out in the news. It was a tragic situation involving Latino parents where the mother murdered her children. The article stated that she was dealing with mental issues and went crazy. One part of the story was overlooked in that article in my opinion. When the mother was questioned about what happened, she said she did it for her husband. When the father walked in the house, the mother told him that the kids would no longer bother him anymore. This was one of the saddest stories I ever read.

I imagine that the father worked long hours and often brought the stress from work home. In doing so, he probably complained and yelled about the noise of his family. While we know that this is normal with children, maybe he didn't. The mother may not have had reliable family members to support her. There is no excuse for what she did but I just wish I could have done something to prevent that.

What resources could have been provided to this family?

What additional support could we have added?

Although I don't speak Spanish, I wish I could have engaged the father somehow. This story tugged at my heart when I was starting out in the field. It made me realize how important the work of family services is. I can't help but think that this couple was never involved with any support programs. Maybe one conversation with the father about co-parenting would have minimized his stress.

This is why setting up ways to engage the entire family is something I will speak about forever. Some may not agree, but I pray for that mother and father. I pray the work we do as service providers will stop situations like that from ever happening again. Most importantly, I pray those little souls are resting in peace.

Hopefully, you are understanding the value of supporting the entire family. I know that we can only do so much but we must do all we can. We never know if we are the only person who is able to get through to a family. We never know how much our personality may affect a person. As social services workers, we are a part of some of these families' lives. For those of you that have been around a while, you know there's no better feeling than helping families elevate. We see them for a while but it's a joyous moment when we don't see them anymore. It's at that moment that we realize we did our job to lift a family out of poverty.

Step 4. Empowering Fathers

"I love being a dad. I love every second of it and I'm not exhausted at all."

- PAUL MCCARTNEY

Fantastic you have made it to the part of the book where it gets more fun than serious. By now you should be thinking about ways to make fathers now view your organization as father friendly. As they are supported there will be opportunities to involve them further. Unlike Paul McCartney in the quote above, fathers do get exhausted. Parenting in general for that matter. Fathers will reach a point where they get overwhelmed. Finding ways to empower is the key to keep them motivated as fathers. Your service organization may play a major role in this process. Now it's time to take things to the next level by empowering the fathers you engage. We will begin with an example of an empowered father

Empowering One Father at a time

It was another day at the WIC office. After interacting and engaging all the fathers that came into the WIC office, I decided to take a lunch break. I grabbed my lunch bag from the break room refrigerator and walked up to the conference room. This is where I would eat lunch, stretch and call my wife before I started the second part of my day. As I was sitting there, I noticed movement at the door. It was my co-worker. She came to tell me that there was a father looking for me. I pointed at my food to say, "I'm eating here." She replied by saying, "This guy seems a little frustrated, I don't think he will wait." So I told her to go ahead and send him up to my office.

When he came in I could tell he was visibly upset. He gave me a stern look and a rough handshake as we met. Will had what I call a natural mean mug. He also had a mouth full of gold teeth like some of the rappers have.

As we sat down at the table I asked him, "What's the problem, my man?".

He whips out a piece of paper and throws it on the table. As I grab the paper I say, "Ok, what's this? And sorry what's your name?"

He tells me his name is Will and goes on to describe the paper. It was a letter from child support services indicating that he must make a payment soon. Will was freaking out because he was concerned about going to jail. He was between jobs a week prior to our meeting but had actually just started working. Because of this, he was late on his payments. As I listened to him, I discovered that Will's main concern was about going to jail for being late on his payment.

I grabbed the letter to review it. Will was exactly right about what the letter was describing and his concerns were legitimate. As I read further, I noticed a small clause at the bottom. It read: "If you cannot make a payment at this time, give us a call to make arrangements for an extension."

After reading that, I looked up at Will. I held the letter up to him and asked if he saw this small writing at the bottom. He said he did but didn't really understand it. I then told him that all he had to do was call the number to get an extension on his payments. I grabbed my phone and started to make the call for him. Will started hyperventilating so much that I had to stand up and check on him.

In a firm voice, I asked, "Are you ok, man?"

He was fine but in a nervous and frightened voice, he said, "Could you please call for me? I don't know how to talk to them people."

This was my first experience with something like this but as a Father Engagement Specialist, I didn't think it was too much for me to do.

After three rings the child support caseworker answered. I started to explain the situation. I told her that I had Will in front of me and he was concerned about his child support payment. I explained how he told me he was unemployed for about a month but had just started working. I told her that Will was concerned about going to jail and is working hard to make a payment. Will watched intently as I spoke on the phone.

The child support worker listened patiently the entire time. In a pleasant voice, she told us that it was ok and that she understands. After that, she notified us that she was going to put an extension on Will's child support payment. She was on speakerphone the entire time so Will could hear her. As she was talking, the look on his face was one of shock and disbelief. As she wrapped up her spiel, Will was sure to tell her to thank you at least ten times.

Once the call was over, he looked at me with tears welling up in his eyes and asked if he could give me a hug. He then came and gave me the biggest bear hug. Overjoyed, he then said, "Thank you so much, Sharmain, you don't know how much this means to me."

As he left, I thought to myself, "What just happened?"

To me, the process of calling the child support worker seemed so simple, but to Will, it was an overwhelming task that might land him in jail.

Think about this: Why didn't Will just call the child support caseworker himself?

Will did not think he would be able to communicate with child support services.

I learned later that Will was intimidated to make the call because of his past experience with child support and how he was incarcerated before. This brought about trust issues. Although it had been a while, in Will's mind he could not trust anyone working with "the system." But he trusted me.

When I engaged him, I did so in an understanding

way and asked more questions than I made declarations. I listened intently as he spoke. We built trust and my nonverbal communication indicated that I cared. Peter Drucker once said, *"The most important thing in communication is hearing what isn't said."*

Recognizing Fathers

This is not about child support or incarceration. What took place next is what this chapter is about. Will instantly joined my program. While in the program, he often volunteered to speak first and share his personal journey. Even after graduation, he continued to come. I had to figure out a way to continue empowering him. So any time there was an event he voluntarily helped set up, tear down and more. I later trained him as a Fatherhood Facilitator and he started being my co-facilitator in groups. One time, I traveled to a speaking engagement and was about to cancel the group. He told me that he would love to lead the group. After signing all his volunteer paperwork, he ran a group session all by himself. I was able to call him right before I went on stage. He was so nervous. I boosted his confidence and he went and did an amazing job.

Empowering the fathers I worked with was the key to the success of the program. As you empower them, they tell their circle of influence and participation increases. This was the case for over a dozen other fathers. We have created a task force for our events now where fathers I met early on, meet to plan out events. At our recent annual Daddy Daughter Dance, six fathers raised funds, promoted, sold tickets, and set up the venue.

I know you are not running a fatherhood program

like I am so you may not have the opportunity to connect like I do. Don't worry, your way of empowering fathers can be totally different. Your volunteer opportunity may come in the form of showing fathers they are essential to the process. For example, at WIC when fathers accompanied mom, we made it our mission to involve dads when it was time to weigh and measure the babies. Since WIC is a nutrition education service, we taught families how to make healthy meals with their food options. We intentionally involved fathers in feeding good healthy snacks to their children. A few times, I hosted a fathers-only cooking session to promote cooking for dads.

These are some small things you may implement. If you are an early head start program, you may do a "reading to your child day" to empower fathers. Let them know you will take a photo or video and share them on your site. If you are in a children's hospital, you may direct questions to dads when he is at the appointment.

When my oldest son was an infant, I attended almost every appointment. One day we had my son's six or twelve month checkup. This was around the same time I was not working so I was essentially a stay-at-home dad. While at the appointment, the nurse asked many questions but she would direct them all to my wife.

"How many stools a day"

"How much is he eating?"

"How many hours does he sleep"

My wife was often tired, as most mothers are with

newborns. With each question asked, my wife would look at me for the answers. I rattled off the answers with hesitation. The nurse finally said to me, "Wow, you are on point, sir! You must really be involved."

I smiled from ear to ear while thinking to myself, "I sure am."

Just those simple words were empowering to me. As a new father with a history of fatherlessness, it felt good to be acknowledged.

As the fatherhood program was running, we made sure we worked with nurse practitioners since we focused on infant mortality. Nurse practitioners would come in and do training on safe sleeping and give away pack-n-plays. We decided to make that session a part of the curriculum. On certain days we would strictly talk about safe sleep.

Recognizing fathers may be the most powerful tool for you to empower fathers. How do I know? Every three months of programming I would have over a dozen graduates. I would host a graduation ceremony for the fathers who completed the course. The ceremony was to celebrate them becoming the best fathers they could be. This was a family event and fathers were encouraged to invite the mother of their children or their current partner. There is always food and music but the highlight is when the fathers speak. Each father prepares a speech to give on stage in front of their family. I usually bring in a speaker or I give a speech myself. This is one of the most empowering moments. Hearing fathers touch on topics that are considered taboo, and watching them express their emotions openly is extremely powerful. These priceless moments are captured on film on my YouTube channel. The ceremony not only recognizes the fathers in the program, it allows their families to recognize them as well.

Acknowledgment and recognition are qualities everyone desires. Studies have shown that employees that are acknowledged and recognized perform better. Through this recognition process, a new light is shined on the fathers that support their performance as men

Volunteer Opportunities

So as you seek to understand, communicate, and support fathers, you will open an avenue to empower them. This will lead to higher engagement as the empowered fathers spread the word about the great people and activities in your organization.

In this step, you want to find those fatherhood champions. If your organization does family events be sure to create volunteer opportunities. Some of the fathers you engage will be stay-at-home fathers as well. Or they are new-age self-employed entrepreneurs who have more flexibility. Don't hesitate to mention an event. Like the nutritionist did with me when I started my career. Who knows, you may have a father come through the program that becomes a candidate for employment.

Increasing Fatherhood Staff

In the prison reentry space, we have a saying: "Those closest to the problem are closest to the solution." When I speak on stage about reentry, I am explaining lived experiences. Also, when I speak to fathers I am speaking from personal experience. A large portion of the fathers in my program literally raised their kids along with me. Their little girls went from running up to me asking about the next dance to becoming volunteers at dances and other events.

Make no mistakes, I am not saying that all family service providers that work with families should be replaced. That would be insensitive and ridiculous. What I am saying is that if there is an opportunity to diversify the workplace you should take advantage of it. I am also not saying you need to hire a father that is a participant. I am just using myself as an example of how that strategy could possibly work. But you may want to hire a person with both personal and technical experience.

Obviously, this is something that involves funding and as a business, you will really need to justify the need in order to allocate resources to it. While there is funding for fatherhood programming, the last I checked it is a narrow avenue. You may have to get creative and find ways to allocate funds alongside other funding sources. For example, since WIC does not do any father-specific programming we could not direct any funds toward it. This included my salary. So we created two positions for one job. I was the WIC and Community Liaison and the Father Involvement Specialist. When I would do outreach, I would be promoting all of the programs WIC had. When I would do presentations, the first part of it would be about WIC. For these activities, I was paid directly by WIC. The WIC budget was much higher so I spent most of my time doing WIC activities. When I would do father-specific programming I would be paid by the smaller funding source supporting the fatherhood program. At the time it was the minority health grant that focused on decreasing infant mortality rates. Notice that this funding source was not specific to fatherhood. Including our work with fathers in our grant proposal put us in a unique position to be rewarded and empower more fathers in our community.

This is something you could consider but you don't have to. You could just provide volunteer opportunities and do well. Someone could volunteer to engage fathers as well. In the next chapter, we will discuss even more creative ways to engage fathers and be seen as a father-friendly organization.

Step 5. Working with Your Community

"You can't achieve anything entirely by yourself. There's a support system that is a basic requirement of human existence. To be happy and successful on earth, you just have to have people that you rely on."

-Michael Schur

You are one step closer to being a top-tier father engagement expert. To be honest, the tools you are learning about don't only apply to fathers. These strategies can be used in all areas of your life.

Let's now look at collaboration and partnerships. This chapter goes right along with empowering and supporting fathers but I wanted to focus on it separately. Whether your organization has the capacity to do father specific programming or not, you will need to collaborate or partner with other organizations for long term sustainability of your efforts.

If there's already a fatherhood organization in your area, it would be a good idea to contact them. If they are already providing direct services to fathers, they could become a referral source. This is an example of collaboration. It could easily turn into a partnership should you apply for a grant and include that organization in your application process. During my time with the Dedicated Dads program, we developed many collaborations and partnerships. For instance, we were the organization providing direct services in the area.

As we grew, the local YMCA expressed interest in our program. They wanted to support our efforts by giving free three and six month memberships for fathers and their families. After strategizing, we developed a partnership. The YMCA applied for a grant and included us in their proposal. We used the YMCA memberships as an incentive for fathers to join the program and the YMCA was able to increase memberships. I imagine the increase in memberships supported the numbers needed to receive other grants.

In the first year of our collaboration, we only did three month memberships. The following year it was increased to six months. As mentioned before, we used the membership initially as an incentive to join. Through trial and error, I discovered that many fathers were enrolling just to get the membership and discontinuing participation shortly after. Like with any program or service, people will try to take advantage. It's not for us to get upset but to simply adjust how we deliver the service. I adjusted by only giving the YMCA memberships to those that completed the program. The time it took to disperse the membership extended but we kept the fidelity of the program.

That was an example of a community partnership that worked great. There were also smaller community partners who supported us. A local football player often donated tickets. We received tickets from the Milwaukee Bucks. Local venues gave us discounts on our fatherhood graduation.

Community partners will enable you to spread awareness of your initiative. You will be invited to resource fairs where you can promote your programs and initiatives. You can share your newly developed marketing material with others and get them on board. As they learn more about what you do they will send referrals over to you. The agencies that will send the most referrals are probations and parole and child support. When I realized this, it bothered me a bit. It's as if you have to be in trouble with the law or economically disadvantaged to receive support. Nevertheless, that is where our social awareness comes in again. We may not be able to affect change everywhere but we can in our area of influence.

As our fatherhood initiative grew, we discovered that the majority of fathers enrolling were non-custodial fathers with child support orders. Child support was one of the first agencies I built a relationship with. I would get so many questions about fathers' rights and the child support process that I had to bring in the child support director at the time. She was promoted but our relationship continued.

This relationship turned into a partnership. The child support program received an Access and Visitation Grant from the State of Wisconsin. They were already running job training and employment programs called Children's First and Elevate. The goal was and still is to support fathers in obtaining gainful employment. The idea is that fathers who are employed can pay their child support. Fathers who pay child support minimize the risk of going to jail. As I stated before, I don't like this concept of debtor prison but I must navigate in the space to reach fathers and families. Our fatherhood program was brought in to provide father specific programming. While great fathers had access to employment pipelines, they still need social and emotional support. What good does it do for someone to seek employment and they are not whole. The smallest issue could trigger them. So our partnership developed. As other funding sources ran out the Access and Visitation grant supported our work in engaging and supporting fathers. This partnership was critical to sustaining our efforts.

This partnership has continued even after I left the *Dedicated Dads* program and started my own company. The community partners you collaborate with may not stretch to the extent we did with the *Dedicated Dads* initiative but hopefully, this example sparks ideas for potential community partners for your organization. The point I want to convey is that this work cannot be done alone.

Community partners have access to resources you don't. Or, your funding sources are explicit to your current services. Don't let that deter you from supporting your families. Where there is a will there's a way. The fact that you have this book shows you are willing. Utilizing these practical steps will help you to make a way and increase father participation in your services. That participation will support the families you serve.

Here are some steps you can take to develop and foster community collaborations and partnerships:

How to Develop Community Collaborations and Partnerships

Community Awareness is Key

The work you are doing is great but everyone needs to know what you are doing. Sure they will hear about it eventually, but you should make sure. One of the first things we did at WIC is gain community awareness. We did this by connecting with our local newspaper. As we got rolling, the newspaper ran a story for everything we did. I know many people don't read paper articles anymore but most news outlets are online now. News outlets are constantly searching for amazing stories. Building some kind of relationship with your local news outlet will bring you attention from people you would never think of.

In the introduction, I shared how my article "Making the Change" increased the participation of fathers. It also got the attention of local elected officials and even the governor. When you have that kind of support, funding opportunities are sure to follow. As you spread awareness of your initiatives, other family services will see the value. Since fatherhood is a family initiative, other family services may want to see where services overlap. To gain a deeper understanding they will ask you to come present to their staff. They may also ask you to be a vendor at a resource fair. In the other stages of your initiative, take full advantage of these opportunities. Not solely for the partnerships with the organization, but for the opportunity to engage more families. Whoever is interested in having you, likely already has a large caseload. There may be some overlap of families as well. That's ok. Although families overlap, your fatherhood initiative is new and the families need to be aware. Not only aware by print marketing or newspaper but by in person genuine connection.

Early in our fatherhood initiative, we connected

with the local preschool. They would have resource day twice a month. This was one of my favorite parts of my job. It allowed me to get from behind the desk and out in the community. Every time I would be a vendor at a resource fair I would recruit at least four or five new fathers. Many times, there were only mothers coming to my booth. I presented to them in the same manner, I would a father. The fathers likely couldn't make it due to work. The mothers would take my information and share it with the father of their children. These resource fairs are the greatest to engage families in your communities. Events like a national night out and other large events are great for recruiting. Also, your local jail or prison often has resource fairs for those returning from incarceration. Being able to make those connections before they are released will resonate greatly with the fathers.

Joining Other Non-profit Boards and Committees

Whether you are in a small community like me or a large metropolitan area, knowing the work of other non-profits is valuable. Non-profit boards change constantly. They are always looking to add new members to bring fresh ideas to the organization. As you start having success, your network will expand. The community will want to know how they can support, partner, and connect families.

Joining other boards is a great way to be aware of the resources out there your fathers could benefit from. KLIHF (Kenosha Lifecourse Initiative for Healthy Families) was a committee I was a part of early on. When we lacked funding to purchase food early on they worked together to provide food at our fatherhood meeting. Another member of the committee is the community director with Anthem Blue Cross and Blue Shield. When we started doing a daddy daughter dance and a Father's Day cookout every year, Anthem was the key sponsor. Gifting us a few thousand dollars for our events. The Boys and Girls Club reached out to us and gave us 20-30 Bucks tickets for the fathers and their kids. This happened a few times.

The point here is that networking is crucial. As a leader, make sure you allow your staff to be involved in other community initiatives. Or even be involved yourself. This strategy brings more resources to the table and more resources support more families.

Master the Art of Storytelling

Throughout this book, I have shared several stories with you. The purpose of telling those stories is for you to gain a deeper understanding. I want you to feel, hear, and smell what is going on with the characters in the story. Our society loves a good story. As you engage fathers, you will develop stories of your own and you will hear the same story told by different people.

If you are the person leading the initiative you will need strong storytelling abilities. Whether the story is told to potential funders or other partners, these stories will add color to the data you are gathering. You may be asked to share your work on a panel discussion at a major conference. This is the time to shine and really speak to the realities of the communities you serve. Your ability to be the voice of the unheard will be invaluable.

You may be thinking, "I'm not a great public speaker." I thought the same at first. One of my first assignments was to speak to a major contributor to our funding source. I was not even working a month yet. I was extremely nervous. I walked in the room and it was filled with people. I was smiling but I was crying on the inside. I stood up to speak and my mind sat down. After introducing myself, the butterflies started to leave. I grew confident and got a standing ovation at the end. Storytelling is not so much about what you say but the conviction in which you say it. As you engage fathers and hear their stories from an emotionally intelligent standpoint, you will become a natural. The story you hear at 8 AM will give you enough content to discuss at your 12 PM meeting. Just like the key for kids to articulate better is reading books, the key to storytelling is listening to stories.

Step 6. Working With Mom

"Remember you are not managing an inconvenience. You are raising a human being."

— KITTIE FRANZ

Throughout this entire book, I have stressed the importance of supporting families. I've told you that the ultimate goal is to strengthen the children. Stating all of that and not speaking about how important mothers are in the process would be an injustice. Since mothers are ideally the parent you will engage first, it's important to understand them as well; more so, their outlook on fatherhood and how they view the importance.

When I was trained by the *National Fatherhood Initiative* to be a Father Engagement Specialist, I was made aware of what's called "Maternal Gatekeeping." The NFI defines it as a mother's protective beliefs about the desirability of the father's involvement in their child's life and the behaviors that either facilitate or hinder co-parenting.

When I talked about my family mediation training before I told you how some young couples don't really know one another so when it comes to custody they don't trust one another. When left unresolved, that mentality in the relationship continues for years. I know a few fathers who have been experiencing co-parenting problems since the child was born and the child is a teen now. I have to remind fathers that deeply seeded emotional issues are involved in any relationship. When you add a child to the mix those emotions intensify. During the group session, I stressed the point about women's emotions. Especially as it relates to post-partum depression. The process of pregnancy and early stages of childbirth are critical for the development of the child. I explained to them that 0-5 is the time where both parents are needed the most. Unfortunately, the message is not always received and a year later I am helping the fathers navigate child support.

There are cultural issues that always tie back into a history of fatherlessness. For example, remember I said that young males tend to learn how to be fathers from their fathers or father's role models. Similarly, young females learn what a father is supposed to be by their fathers or father's role model. In the absence of positive male father figures, young couples are on their own. They create what they think is a relationship based on the culture they grew up in. To take it a little further, the mothers raising the young girls have a great influence on them. Imagine this mother's father was not present in her life and her child's father (her daughter's father) is currently not in her life. She now teaches her daughter everything she knows about dealing with this situation.

In my position it's interesting. I will get calls from mothers of teens for both young men and women. For the young women, the mothers (Grandmas) contact me to reach out to the father. They hope I can get through to him. For the young men, the mothers (Grandma) call me to help the son navigate child support, get more time with his child or teach him about co-parenting. A few times, separate grandmothers of the same grand-child have called me.

I highlight this for you to understand the complexities. As you understand the challenges you will know how to work through them. Trust me, I know it's not entirely our job to get involved in these scenarios but when you understand the mindset it supports you in doing your job.

Let's look at three common reasons for Maternal Gatekeeping.

1. (Anger) Mom and Dad are no longer romanti-cally involved.

This is probably the most challenging, especially with young couples. They already don't fully under-stand themselves but now they are trying to understand a partner and a baby. When these situations happen it's often because the father moved on. I put the screws to the fathers I work with when we talk. As a guy, I know we are raised to be smooth talkers and say what needs to be said. Is this right? No, but it's real. Kids in school are not taught how to make healthy relationship decisions. Relationship advice is not taught at all if you ask me. But if you go to any middle school, you will see kids in relationships. So they don't know how relationships work which means they definitely don't know how to break up.

Think about it. Our environment taught us how to get into a relationship but were you ever taught how to end a relationship? Probably not... Now think about trying to break up when a child is involved. A few times I have tried to do a young parent's co-parenting session. Every time, I had zero attendance. Like many of us, pride is thick in our minds early in life. It is only through experiential learning that we start to grow.

2.   A father is not paying child support.

You read about how some fathers withhold as a bargaining chip to see their children early. This is the other side of the coin. I am so glad to see changes in child support services because the older culture focused only on forcing a person to pay child support. Send them to jail and then they don't pay. This is why I am not anti-child support, I'm anti-going to jail for child support. I never understood how that even became law. Sadly, in some cases, child support payments and interest continue when a father is incarcerated. How will he pay? One time, I sat down with a father who served ten years in federal prison. His child support order continued the entire time. His balance was over $150,000 once released. If you thought to yourself, "That is crazy," you are right.

Anyhow, I didn't mean to get off track but the system is in serious need of an upgrade. Going back to a father not paying child support. Check out this scenario:

A couple breaks up and then the father moves on. Emotions run high and the mother no longer allows him to see the child. The father finds a way to get in court to gain more access and visitation. The courts now know the couple is not together and increase child support. Father is ok with that as long as his visitation increases. He is granted more time but the mother is not happy about it. Although there are set times, the mother continues to withhold the child. The father tries going back to court and no consequences are given to the mother. She is only told she must follow the order. Despite going through court twice, the mother still does not follow the order. Now the dad, not understanding the process, withholds his child support payments. He thinks that he can argue this point in court. They go to court and the father argues that since he is not seeing his child he did not pay child support. He doesn't know that the courts don't care and is sent to jail for a six-month sentence.

Father then loses his job that allowed him to pay child support in the first place. He also loses his apartment amongst other things. His time inside scarred him since it was his first time in jail. He no longer trusts the system or his child's mother. If going to jail is the consequence of being a stand up father trying to do what's right, he may as well just stay away from it all. Just pay child support and dismiss visitation. Fathers who do this are often called dead beats. The reality is, they were beaten dead by the family courts. Through that entire scenario, no one thought about the impact on the child. Another child going through emotional and financial instability.

Someone may say it's not the family court's job to fix relationships and I totally agree. Once a couple reaches the courts it is the tip of the iceberg. Below the iceberg is everything mentioned so far in this book. Hopefully, you can begin to see the tip and notice things below.

I'm not saying you have to jump in the water and melt the ice yourself. I am asking you to be life support or safety net that helps these couples get to shallower waters. As you continue the work, more families will make decisions on dry land and the children will avoid the deeply emotional, mental, and financial waters that drown many of them.

3. Fear of losing benefits from other programs when reporting household income.

Again, most programs cater to single mothers. Income guidelines make families ineligible for assistance. Mothers learn that they must appear to be single in order to receive service. You and I know this is not true for every program and guidelines are different for each program. Unfortunately, most believe all programs are interwoven together. On several occasions at WIC, I have witnessed mothers I knew personally tell staff that there was not a father involved. These would be situations where mother and father are no longer romantically involved. Interestingly enough, I would know the father was involved in the child's life because he was involved in my program. Since the funding sources for fathers were separate from WIC, no conflict would arise had the mother said he was involved. Because she believed all programs are connected she chose to say he was not involved.

The same goes for most schools. Mothers are usually the ones that fill out paperwork. They may check the box for single moms because they think the school would report the father. Dad is probably the person picking the kids up from school but the data shows he is not involved.

For this reason, we have to be careful of how we interpret statistics on fatherlessness. Most statistics say X percentage of children grew up without fathers in the "household." The stats are true but consider how the information is gathered. Mothers may be asked, "Does Dad live with you?" If she says no, then that data is recorded. A fairer question to ask is: "Is dad involved with the children?" Fathers may not be in the household but he may be very much involved.

The reasons for Maternal Gatekeeping are especially true for fathers with felonies. Public housing laws ensure that felons can't live in a house that receives assistance. This gives even more reason for mothers to deny involvement in theory and in practicality.

I want to share a study I did at WIC to help you understand this idea more. I was in the process of creating a plan to involve my mothers in recruitment. I wanted to know how they felt about father involvement and get a glimpse of their viewpoint. I asked five questions.

Q1. Father involvement is important to the life of my child.

Q2. My child's father needs to be more involved in my child's life.

Q3. There are barriers to my child's father being involved in my child's life.

Q4. I see the benefit of having my child's father involved in WIC's nutrition program

Q5. I'm willing to encourage my child's father to

get involved in the Fatherhood Program

I gathered a lot of quantitative data but for the purpose of this book, we will look at the qualitative data provided by the commentary. The comments were great for the most part but there are a few comments that help you understand the complexities of Maternal Gatekeeping.

A survey done with 103 mothers at WIC.

Q1. Father involvement is important to the life of my child.

"If the father is cooperative and nice to the mother and child."

"Yes, a father's involvement is very important to the child(ren). It prevents a lot of things from going on in their lives."

"Yes, in every aspect."

"If they aren't just going to be there part-time."

"The father plays a very important role the mother can't and vice versa."

"If the father puts in the effort."

"I believe a child is supposed to have both parents."

"Mentally healthy families create happy children."

"It depends on the family situation."

As you can see, some of the comments are fair while others are not. The purpose of showing you this is to highlight some of the reasons for Maternal Gatekeeping, as well as how many mothers view father involvement to be important. Notice how the word "if" is used by the mothers who don't agree. Most of the "if" dealt with issues with themselves or issues with the fathers. The one "if" I agree with is the one about the father being part time. Absolutely, but who defines the time spent with the children? Again, the survey gives you an understanding of how some mothers think. Both positive and negative.

Working with mothers will take a level of understanding just like working with dad. Ultimately, you will understand the family dynamic of the families you serve and you will be well equipped to support them.

Q2. My child's father needs to be more involved in my child's life.

"He's very involved."

"My husband is a great father to all of the children."

"The other kid's father is not involved."

"We need to find him first."

"My child's father is very involved. He is a good dad."

"We live together."

"It's important for a son to have his father in his life all the time, not just when he wants to be."

"He has been missing from my kid's life since my daughter was a year and since the day my son was born."

"My kid's fathers has been involved in their life every day but I do agree, father's need to be more involved."

"He has not even met him."

"Can't force someone to want to take care of their responsibilities."

"My son's father is in the picture; my unborn child's father is not."

"Their dad is very involved."

"He has to take care of himself until he is stable enough."

As you read the comments, how do they make you feel? I get mixed feelings. As I was doing the survey I was elated to see how many mothers saw the value. I will be honest, my implicit bias blinded me. In addition, the survey highlighted the complexities of fatherhood even more. One comment said, *"The other kid's father is not involved."* This is a stepparent scenario. The same with this comment *"My son's father is in the picture, my unborn child's father is not."* So think about the child who watches their siblings' father be involved and their father is not. I remember when my teenage stepdaughter was about seven. I walked into the living room to find her whimpering quietly. I asked her what was wrong and she burst out in tears. I sat down on the couch with her and she gave me a hug. Her biological father had lied to her again. He told her he was coming to see her but never did. She internalized this and started believing she was the problem. As she told me that, tears welled in my eyes. I held her as tight as I could and quietly said, "I will always be here for you." To this day, this is a rough issue as the father still battles adversity. On one hand, I am upset because my daughter is sixteen and he is missing out on precious moments. On the other hand, I know he can turn it around just like many of the fathers I engage.

Q3. There are barriers to my child's father being involved in my child's life.

"He is very emotionally abusive to me."

"We can't agree on anything."

"Their father is in prison for twenty-nine years."

"He just chooses not to come around."

"My child's father is very involved."

"There should be no barriers between a child and their father."

"I do not want him anywhere near my children by any means."

"There are daily barriers that keep many fathers from being involved but many fathers still take the time to be involved as much as possible."

"He has warrants out for his arrest and I have a restraining order on him."

First off, domestic violence is real and the male is the culprit more often than not. Like I said before young people are not taught how to develop relationships and definitely not how to end one. This is why I used the *Nurturing Father's Curriculum*. It uses the adult adolescent parenting inventory that assesses the parenting and child rearing attitudes of adolescents and adult parents and pre-parent populations. It focuses on five key areas.

- Expectations of Children

- Parental Empathy Towards Children's Needs

- Use of Corporal Punishment

- Parent-Child Family Roles

- Children's Power and Independence

Domestic violence (DV) should be taken seriously. Through the program, I discovered that DV is sometimes cultural and has its roots in fatherhood as well. If someone saw violence in their home, they may think it's normal. Addressing this is an essential part of my program to this day.

Q4. I see the benefit of having my child's father being involved in WIC's nutrition program.

"He doesn't live with me, so his involvement isn't necessary."

"I don't see it necessary for him to be involved in WIC's nutrition program but it's important for him to be involved in nutrition in general."

"It's up to him if he wants to be involved."

"He does all of the shopping and most of the WIC pickups."

"I do not want him involved."

Pay attention to the first comment. I can assure you that the only reason that comment was made was because of her belief about social programs. She said he was not involved because of the fear of losing benefits. The second comment as well. Now, look at the last comment. "I do not want him involved." The mother felt she had the power to have him involved.

Q5. I'm willing to encourage my child's father to get involved in the Fatherhood Program.

"He is very busy and involved with the program already."

"My son has a father figure who would love to be involved."

"I encourage it."

"He has completed the WIC father group and is still involved."

"He does need more support, however, I do not talk to him."

The comments in the last questions are what inspired me to excel in my profession. Hearing feedback like this was powerful. Especially to hear that the mother thought the father needed more support even though she does not talk to him. The effects of Maternal Gatekeeping are too critical to not address. Some mothers are now even aware of what they are doing. The effects of Maternal Gatekeeping include but are not limited to:

- Threatening the overall well-being and adjustment of the child in the short term and long term

- Difficulties for the child to adjust to parental divorce or separation

- Damaging the father-child relationship

- Damaging the mother-child relationship

- Damaging the parents' relationship and ability to effectively co-parent

Working with moms was the key to working with dads for me at WIC.

If your organization is not currently intentional about involving fathers this may be a heavy lift. No worries, as the mothers you serve notice how you are prioritizing fathers, they will adjust. You will have great success working with moms who value fatherhood. You will also notice the gates to Maternal Gatekeeping beginning to lower. Although these are serious and complex issues, your organization will play a role in changing the narrative.

What are some of the problems the mothers you work with have involving fathers? I'm sure you can come up with a list. Here are some practical steps to address them:

How To Work With Moms

When I discuss the topic of co-parenting with fathers in a group it is always an emotion driven lesson. Several times I have hosted co-parenting sessions and I found this to be challenging with so many different sets of parents. My one-on-one co-parenting sessions are great, but attendance for group sessions is often low. Because of that, I started hosting co-parenting sessions with mothers who were not romantically involved with any of the fathers in the group. These sessions were long and fruitful. Both men and women were able to see other perspectives from the opposite sex and apply lessons with their partners.

You may start something similar. At a minimum, you can start a mom's group. These groups will give you opportunities to uncover some of the deeper needs of mothers and support them. As you gain trust, you can emphasize the importance of a healthy family.

Here are some themes or topics you can use during discussions:

- Stress the importance of putting the well-being of the child first when talking to mothers

- Stress the importance of mutual respect (i.e. importance of mom respecting dad and vice versa)

- Provide education on co-parenting

- Provide education on conflict resolution

Step 7. Strengthening Families

"There's so much negative imagery of black fatherhood. I've got tons of friends that are doing the right thing by their kids, and doing the right thing as a father - and how come that's not as newsworthy?"

- WILL SMITH

As a formerly incarcerated father, I am often told I have a chip on my shoulder. I say, "Rightfully so." One of the best things about going through the justice system is that you learn about it. As I studied historical policies and researched historical laws that gravely impacted families, that chip grew larger. When you think about how many fathers are incarcerated for victimless crimes you understand why there is a generation of fatherlessness. My mission in life is to support all fathers but I am intentional about formerly incarcerated fathers.

Men make up 90 percent of incarcerated people of which the majority are fathers. Fathers that are predominantly men of color. Over 600,000 people are released from prison every year. Many of them are fathers who will come into your support services in need of help. Although they have parole agents who provide them with resources, they don't always trust them. The fathers may also have child support orders, and in some instances, failing to keep up with child support payments is a parole violation. Additionally, recidivism rates remain constant although crime rates decrease.

Fredrick Douglas said, "It is easier to build strong children than to repair broken men." While I agree with this quote, I don't give up on trying to repair broken men. Those men are still children in the eyes of their parents. They are the champions in their children's lives. The smallest shift in the mind of these fathers can have the greatest impact on them like it did with me. That has been the spirit of my approach with every father I work with. Father involvement during the reentry process has been proven to strengthen families. I would be remiss if I didn't stress this point.

Father Involvement and Reentry

According to several researchers, understanding fathers' reentry process and their involvement with their children during this period is important. This importance comes not only because of the key role fathers play in the lives of their children, but also the burgeoning literature that correlates numerous negative child outcomes, such as poorer health, academic, social, and behavioral outcomes in addition to aspects of cumulative disadvantage such as poverty, residential instability, and food insecurity (Maruschak, Glaze, and Mumola 2010; Gorman-Smith, Grisa Hunt, and Roberston 2012; Choi, Palmer, and Pyun 2014; Wildeman, Haskins, and Poehlmann-Tynan 2017; Turney 2018.).

Equally important, the literature identifies the father-child relationship as a protective factor in reducing recidivism rates for fathers reentering the community after incarceration. (Bahr et al. 2005;

Visher, Bakken, and Gunter 2013.). Yet, evidence also suggests that, despite their forced separation from their families while in prison, incarcerated fathers believe parenthood is a key facet of their self-identity (Meek 2011). Researchers identify the quality of father-child relationships maintained during paternal incarceration as a key predictor of relationship quality upon the father's reentry (Festen et al. 2002).

In addition, fathers reported that spending time with their children was a prominent reason for staying out of prison, with many indicating that they considered their relationship with their children as a deterrent to behaviors that could lead to arrest (Visher and Courtney 2007). This mindset has been substantiated by research that finds lower rates of reincarceration among fathers who had contact with their children while in prison and those who had positive relationships with their children after release (Bahr et al. 2005; Bales and Mears 2008; Derkzen, Gobeil, and Gileno 2009; Duwe and Clark 2011).

An increasing number of studies discussing paternal incarceration and reentry have been published in recent years (e.g., Fowler et al. 2017; McLeod and Bonsu 2018; McLeod and Gottlieb 2018), most of which close with policy and practice recommendations suggesting that reentry should be viewed as an ongoing process from the first day of one's incarceration and that those supporting reentry should constantly be embracing strategies to reinforce parent-child bonds and preparing fathers for their inevitable return to the community (Crandell-Williams and McEvoy 2017).

The lack of reentry preparation likely contributes

to increased recidivism and, in the case of fathers, reduced parental self-efficacy and father involvement (Sabol, West, and Cooper 2009).

There are many great reentry programs educating fathers about substance abuse, mental health, job readiness, and employment. I think that is great, but the topic of fatherhood speaks to the heart of the fatherless. I strongly believe that if you can get a man to see the value of fatherhood and the long term impact it can have on his children, everything else will naturally align. Knowing his children are affected by every decision he makes will force him to think differently. Like me, when he discovers how long certain communities have fallen victim to unjust policies, he will seek to rise above it. By supporting fathers, you are indeed supporting families.

When I entered the military-based prison boot camp program I didn't know what to expect. All I knew was that completing the six-month program would reduce my five year sentence in half. The program challenged me both physically and mentally. Constant physical training, programming, and work gave me the discipline I wish I had before I went to prison. Toward the end of the program, I found out about another group through a Sgt. who dedicated his time to this group.

The group's focus was on fatherhood and being a responsible man. We used the book *The Resolution of Men* by Authors Alex and Stephen Kendrick and Randy Alcorn. The book focuses on challenging men to reconcile with their pasts; re-engage in the present by taking full responsibility for their wives and children, and move forward with a bold resolution for the future. We also watched the movie *Courageous* written and directed by the same authors. The story was about everyday heroes who long to be the kinds of dads that make a lifelong impact on their children. Since it was religious based, the group was completely voluntary. Although my biological son was not yet born, this group, book, and a movie changed my life forever. I didn't realize it at the time but God was preparing me for something greater. Everything I had been through in the streets, courts, and prison was the foundation for what I was called to do. The group gave me the fire to be bold and courageous in the fight for fatherhood.

If you have not seen the movie *Courageous* yet, I highly recommend you watch it with your family. Although it is deeply religious, the principles can apply to any father or family.

I know this is a tall order and the work you do already is challenging enough but we are called to be courageous in everything we do. You can and will be courageous as you strengthen and build the fathers in your services. Some of you younger professionals may not have children of your own. You may think you can't make an impact. You can and you will. Your voice and experience working with families is invaluable. When you are able to tell the stories of others from a personal view, others have no choice but to respect it. I challenge you to think about what kind of society you want your children in when you do have some. Strong and healthy families have always been the backbone of our nation. Unfortunately, there are some major forces that don't realize that. We do our nation a disservice if we stand back and do nothing. The time is now for us to stand in the gaps and do the work that needs to be done to raise strong families and strong communities.

Conclusion

"I am not going to bury my son. My son is going to bury me."

DENZEL WASHINGTON - John Quincy Archibald

The movie *John Q,* starring Denzel Washington, depicted an amazing show of co-parenting. After the couple's son collapses at his baseball game they rush to the hospital. It's discovered that the boy's heart is twice the average size it should be. After several days in the hospital, the parents are notified that the insurance would no longer cover the procedures needed to save the boy's life. The scene that stood out the most to me was when the mother called the father on the payphone to explain the situation. In a panicked voice, she yelled, "Do something, John!" Hearing his wife in so much grief, John took action by holding the doctor's hostage. Police were called, swat teams positioned themselves as John held doctors in one room. He was going to force them to operate.

After the doctors told the father there was nothing they could do, the father threatened to kill himself. He told them to use his heart for his son. The scene is very intense and emotional. The doctors eventually operated and saved the boy's life. John went to jail but he went gracefully as he knew he sacrificed for his son.

What I am highlighting is the way the mother and

father worked together to fight for their son. Imagine if the mother was there alone dealing with that situation. She may not have been able to handle it. Imagine if the father was there alone, he could have handled it worse than he did.

At the end of 2018, my wife and I found out we were pregnant with our third child. We were excited and hoping for a girl. Although I was blessed with a stepdaughter, I wondered what it would be like to raise a girl from birth. About four months into the pregnancy, my wife and I hosted a gender reveal party. To our surprise, God blessed us with another son. My daughter and son were excited to have another brother coming. Then things took a scary turn. One night, my wife woke me up and said something did not feel right. I didn't think too much of it. I just thought it was regular pregnancy pains. Then she said the same thing again in a more serious tone.

"Something doesn't feel right."

She sat on the toilet as she grimaced in pain. I checked on her and noticed the toilet was filled with blood. Shocked, I said, "We have to go to the ER."

We gathered our things and headed straight to the ER. When we went there and explained the situation, the nurses were urgent but said these were common. This pregnancy may be a high risk pregnancy they said. They assured us they could take steps to hold off delivery but at some point my wife could be on bed rest. My wife and I prayed as we waited for the nurse to come back and do an examination.

The nurse came back and started examining my

wife. With a puzzled look on her face, she told us she may need to get an x-ray. She started examining again then she stepped out of the room. When she came back she was with another nurse. A more senior nurse. My wife said, "What is going on?" I stood and said the same.

They ordered an x-ray that came almost immediately. The nurse left again. All of a sudden the nurses rushed back in and said, "We have to get you to deliver, you are ten centimeters dilated!"

My wife instantly cried out, "Oh no God, please don't let me miscarry."

She was only about twenty-four weeks into the pregnancy at the time. She cried even louder as they rolled her down the hallway. I was guided to the waiting room. A nurse stayed to comfort me and explain what was happening in real-time.

As I sat in the room, I called my father and mother in law. Overwhelmed with fear, I cried to them as I waited.

A nurse came back into the room after what felt like hours. With a smile on her face, she said the baby is ok. All I could think to myself was thank God. Then she confused me when she said, "He was born 1 pound and 10 ounces."

"Oh, he was born?" I replied in shock.

She told me that they would need to take him to a Milwaukee hospital where he could be taken care of better.

My wife and son were escorted in an ambulance

as I drove up. Mixed emotions ran through me. I have heard stories about premature babies not surviving and having complications. I didn't know what to expect.

Over the next six to twelve months, my wife and I would experience the biggest challenge of our lives. Our son had great difficulties. His breathing alarms constantly went off. They had to pump him up with all the pain medication you could think of. He needed twenty-four-hour care. For the first week, we stayed at the hospital with him. But we could not live at the hospital.

We still had lives and two other kids to care for. On top of that, we had just closed on our first house a month before my son was born. My wife stopped working her job for a while and I had to use all of my hours and family leaves hours. Financial, emotional, and spiritual stress took a toll on us. I was also at the end of my bachelor's degree program at Carthage College.

We were on the phone constantly. At least three or four times we were called in the middle of the night and told that our son was dying. I would drive in silence as my wife balled her eyes out. At one point, the doctors came to us and asked us to consider the option of letting my son die. My son had heavy bleeding in his brain at the time and was at risk for major complications. This was absolutely not an option for us. At least, we were not going to be the ones to decide his fate. If God called him, then so be it. I told the doctor that we wanted them to do everything they could to save him. We are ok with him having some kind of disability.

At one point, it became too overwhelming for my wife and she wanted to give up. She didn't want to see our son go through so much pain. Although I felt the same deep inside, I did not let her see that. I instructed the doctors to only talk to me and to call me for the next week as my wife battled with the reality of things. For some reason, this was not received well. My awareness of father alienation heightened my senses to disrespect.

A few times, I had to stand firm and speak loud and clear to staff. I lost all of my religion at one point. I did not care. Like John Q, I knew it was my duty to do everything in my power to save my son's life.

Over the next two months, we would travel back and forth from Kenosha to Milwaukee for our son. My family and friends came to visit and pray. My father came often to pray over my son.

One night we were called and told he was shipped to Children's Hospital. Not for complications but to support him better. Things seemed to get better from there. The social worker told us about the Ronald McDonald house. My wife stayed there for a few weeks as I worked and cared for our thirteen and five year olds. The social worker also provided us with other resources like Social Security, health insurance, and support programs. The social worker was very comfortable and confident talking to me. After talking to her and getting the resources, my wife and I had a sense of relief. Although it wasn't much, Social Security helped offset some expenses.

My son eventually came home on oxygen support. He also had a gestational tube in his stomach for feeding. The time after the hospital was even more challenging. At least once a week we had to travel back to Children's Hospital. A few times we were readmitted.

The whole time, I never gave up on my faith that God would see us through.

I continued to host fatherhood groups weekly. Only, this time, I relied on the fathers for support. The fathers who I had been teaching were now the ones supporting me. The community stepped up in a major way as I used crowdfunding to help with our expenses. My co-workers raised funds, gave gift cards, and more. One of my co-workers paid my mortgage for a month. My supervisor and a college professor were very understanding.

Not long after all of this, the Covid-19 pandemic came. All in person therapy for my son stopped. We were fearful of going to hospitals. They made a rule that only one parent could attend sessions. This infuriated me. My spirit was not settled until my wife looked at me and said, "I got it, honey." She was letting me know that she could handle herself.

Fast forward to now, my son is well and healthy. He is two years old and has no major complications. He is just a bit behind in development due to prematurity. My wife handles all of the appointments now. She amazes me at how she advocates for our son's health. I trust everything she says when it comes to his care. During this entire journey, we had to work together.

In this story, did you see how both my wife and I had to work together for our son?

Did you see how as a father I had to step in for my wife when she was at a low point?

Do you see how she later stepped up for me?

What about the social worker? Notice how efficient she was?

Notice my view on the nurses and doctors and how there was a bit of tension there.

While much of the story was about my wife and I, the support around us is the greater lesson. Our struggles would have been worse without the support. Not just from professionals, but from family, friends, and co-workers as well.

The community in which we lived stepped up for us in our greatest time of need. You are part of the community you live in and the families around you could use your support.

After going through all of that with the hospital, I began to research more. Think about how many single mothers may go into hospital with high risk pregnancies. As I stated, the state of Wisconsin has the highest infant mortality rates. I wonder how many of those are from pressure or lack of understanding of professionals. Fortunately, for my wife and I, I was educated and fearless. Imagine how many mothers may choose to give up and "let their child go." This is nothing personal against health care providers. They have a job to do. I know the doctors simply needed to communicate the risk to me so that I could make an informed decision. But what if my wife was alone? What if she made a decision without me? What if she did not have me as a father in her corner to support her? What if I was not around at all?

Both the movie *John Q* and my story are extreme, but things like this happen every day in communities.

The well-being of children is always better decided by both parents. When I speak to the fathers I inform them how doing everything they can for their kids is the only option. Speaking up for their children when they can't, fighting on their behalf and advocating for them every chance they get. Not to the extreme of Denzel Washington's character but they get the point. In the hospital, I had to fight for my son and I will do so until I die.

My wife and I at the hospital with our premature son

A while back I found research saying that if a child is not reading by third grade they will possibly go to prison. My son has been reading since he was four. I have to fight for my son. Not long ago, my daughter was suspended after being bullied. My wife and I went to the school immediately to examine the situation. My daughter reported the bully twice and nothing was done. Since I knew how processes should work, I challenged them on their protocol. It was deemed that they did not handle it correctly and my daughter's suspension was removed. We had to fight for her.

As service providers, we may not be able to mend relationships but we can surely talk about the benefits of a two-parent relationship for the children and help parents make informed decisions. We can provide resources, send referrals, and go the extra mile. We can talk about the impacts of fatherlessness. We can stress the importance of taking care of the entire family and not just women, infants, and children.

Working at WIC really opened my eyes to how families should be supported. Looking back on our Father's Involvement Initiative, I realize that the problem was never that the fathers didn't want to come in to receive services. The problem was they didn't think they could. According to research, black fathers are the most involved fathers up until age five. What happens at age five? The children start going to school. I am not saying schools are separating families, just pointing out a fact. Many fathers don't think they need to be involved at school as well. Most just simply pick them up and drop them off. The fathers I work with are taught to send emails to all of the teachers introducing themselves so the teachers know them. Like fathers, teachers need support as well.

Fathers are more involved than ever before and need just as much support as mothers do. This brings balance to the family and ultimately supports the children. The children are the next generation of our country. It is on people like you and me to be a driving force in this fight for families. It's on us to ensure that our future is strong. When they write the history books, it will include more than information about wars, pandemics, and stock market crashes. It will show us that family service providers stood TALL for our own families and the families we work with!

STAND TALL

Now that you have this information what will you do?

How dedicated are you to supporting healthy families?

What steps can you implement immediately to become a more father-friendly organization?

What can you do right now to make an impact?

Next Steps

If you made it to this part of the book, congratulations! You are dedicated to the cause of building and strengthening families through father involvement. I know this was a lot of information to consume at once and you may feel overwhelmed but in a good way. You are ready to go out and change the world. You are not alone!

Since I started my own company, I have traveled the country giving keynote presentations, training and workshops to organizations serving fathers and formerly incarcerated people. My mission is to help fathers and families flourish one city at a time. I would love the opportunity to connect with you and support you on your journey.

I also recently developed a one of a kind fatherhood

program called *The Fatherhood Franchise Program* (TFFP).

The program provides social, emotional, and mental support to this group of fathers as they overcome the challenges of reentry and child custody. TFFP also provides education and resources to help fathers achieve educational, career, and financial goals.

As a result of the Covid-19 pandemic, I recently converted all of my training to an online format so that I can serve fathers all over the world.

My program gives fathers the tools and skills needed to go from good to great fathers.

My platform is something that is easily accessible to any fatherhood population. Visit fatherhoodfranchise.com and join my email list to learn more.

Additionally, I am a Nurturing *Fathers Curriculum* trainer. I offer this service to organizations that are considering using the curriculum to support the fathers in their program. So if you have a candidate in mind that will take the lead on father engagement we can get them prepared.

Finally, I know many of you reading this spend a lot of time dealing with processes and protocol. Sometimes you can get overwhelmed. Some professionals begin to view people simply as case numbers and caseloads. In my presentations and workshops, I helped professionals take a deep dive into human centered design frameworks around engaging fathers. I would love to connect with you to provide more information.

From now on, consider me your coach, guide, consultant, and mentor in this journey to support fathers and families.

If you would like to connect more, contact me by email at info@workingwithdads.com

Thank you!

Acknowledgments

I would like to express my thanks and gratitude to the people who helped me in writing this book.

First and foremost, I want to thank God, who has been with me in my entire journey in life. In those times when I felt alone, you comforted me.

To my father, Monroe Mitchell; I didn't understand what you were doing when I was young but now I do. Your strength and resilience are the greatest traits I inherited from you. You never gave up on me. Even when I got out of line, you always showed love and compassion.

To my mother: Mom, you are the strongest person I know. Raising five children with little help is powerful. I know our upbringing was tough but you made a "way" out of "no way." You always tell me "Greatness Always, Son." You give me the drive I need to be great in life.

To the Racine/Kenosha Community Action Agency/WIC: Thank you for taking a chance on me. I honestly still can't believe you hired me. I can't believe that our work has risen to this level. I remember asking, "Why did you hire me?" and you said, "Because of your passion." That passion is something I promise to keep as I continue in the work of fatherhood.

To my daughter, Raziya. When I met you, you were five. I am grateful to have you in my life. You prepared me to be a father. While in prison, you wrote me a letter that said, "Things are not the same now that you are not here, Daddy." I keep that letter to this day as a reminder to continue on. You are the secret to all my success. I love you.

A special thanks to all the fathers I work with over the years. Without your participation, I would not be where I am today.

Most importantly, I would like to acknowledge my wife, Shanika; I can't thank you enough. You were there the entire time I was in prison. You sent me money from your income tax checks to support me. You answered every phone call and were right there when I was released. You gave birth to my son and that changed my life. You showed me how to be a better man. While I pursue my career, you have been supporting me by taking care of our children. I know the time I spent away was stressful but it was all for a higher purpose.

My Family

About the Author

Sharmain Harris is a national speaker and trainer on father engagement and prison reentry. After spending three years incarcerated, Sharmain worked hard to overcome the barriers to successful reentry into society. Prior to being a speaker, he worked at WIC as a Father Engagement Specialist. He is known for taking a fatherhood initiative from grassroots to being known nationally. For his work, Sharmain was awarded the NAACP Positive Impact Award, the 20 under 40 Award, and Excellence in Community Action Award.

He credits the birth of his first biological child for giving him meaning and purpose in life. His turnaround story is one of perseverance, resilience, and dedication. A graduate of Carthage College, he lives in Kenosha, WI, with his wife and three children.

www.ingramcontent.com/pod-product-compliance
Lightning Source LLC
Chambersburg PA
CBHW031521270326
41930CB00006B/475